大学生のための
国際教養
ハンドブック

A Handbook of
International Understanding for
University Students

編著 竹野純一郎
　　　Junichiro Takeno
著　 佐生 武彦
　　　Takehiko Saiki

ふくろう出版

読者の皆さんへ

　本書には、14章の対話文と付録の読み物が収録されています。読み物はすべて、大学教員であるProfessor Saikiと大学生であるEriの2人による会話形式をとっています。内容的には主に大学生に知っておいてもらいたい事柄や考えてもらいたい題材を選んであるので、単なる英会話教本というよりは、各章が扱っているトピックについて考えを深める教養本としての役割もあると考えています。比較的読みやすい内容のものから、考えさせられるであろう内容のものまでバラエティ豊かなトピックを選びましたが、本書を読む際には、教員や学生の立場になり、想像力を働かせ、積極的な姿勢で読んでほしいと思います。書かれていることをただ受け入れるのではなく、批判的に読むことも大切な心構えだと考えています。

　本書は、中国学園大学国際教養学部の佐生武彦先生との共著になります。佐生先生とは、私が中国学園に赴任してからの9年間、一緒にお仕事をさせていただいています。現在の中国学園大学国際教養学部で勤務する以前の中国短期大学英語コミュニケーション学科時代から、「一緒に教材の執筆をしよう」と言っていただいていましたので、やっと念願がかなったことになります。佐生先生はアメリカで長期の留学経験があり、異文化コミュニケーションの造詣が深く、大変な読書愛好家で、英語劇団の座長を務められており、音楽愛好家かつバンドマンであり、人間味あふれる愛嬌たっぷりな現中国学園大学国際教養学部の学部長です。佐生先生と共著で本書を出版できることを、編著者としてとても嬉しく思います。

　最後になりましたが、今回の出版に際して、全編の校正だけでなく編集にも関わってくれた同僚の森年ポール氏に厚く御礼を申し上げます。また、本書の出版にあたっては、ふくろう出版の亀山裕幸氏に大変お世話になりました。心より御礼申し上げます。『大学生のための国際教養ハンドブック』が、大学生や英語学習者にとって、一歩踏み込んだ少し教養のある会話を英語でできるようになる一助になることを願っています。

＊本書は平成28・29年度中国学園特別研究助成により、出版経費の一部助成を受けて刊行したものです。

平成30年3月15日
編著者　竹野純一郎

A Handbook of International Understanding
for University Students

大学生のための国際教養ハンドブック

Contents

Chapter 1   English Communication (1) ... 1
            SAIKI, Takehiko

Chapter 2   English Communication (2) ... 4
            SAIKI, Takehiko

Chapter 3   Studying Abroad ... 7
            TAKENO, Junichiro

Chapter 4   The Necessity of English ... 10
            TAKENO, Junichiro

Chapter 5   The Dominance of English ... 13
            TAKENO, Junichiro

Chapter 6   Culture and Civilization (1) ... 17
            SAIKI, Takehiko

Chapter 7   Culture and Civilization (2) ... 20
            SAIKI, Takehiko

Chapter 8   The Importance of Presentation Skills ... 23
            TAKENO, Junichiro

Chapter 9   Travel and Tourism ... 26
            TAKENO, Junichiro

Chapter 10 Art Appreciation ... 29
            TAKENO, Junichiro

Chapter 11 Religions ... 32
            TAKENO, Junichiro

Chapter 12 On Cultural Relativism (1) ... 35
            SAIKI, Takehiko

Chapter 13 On Cultural Relativism (2) ... 38
            SAIKI, Takehiko

Chapter 14 On Cultural Relativism (3) ... 41
            SAIKI, Takehiko

Supplementary Reading   A Sound Historical Perspective ... 44
            SAIKI, Takehiko

Chapter 1

English Communication (1)

This is a conversation between Professor Saiki and a student called Eri. They are talking about communication in English.

Eri: Professor Saiki, I really want to improve my English skills during the first three semesters at this university.

Professor: That means you plan to participate in our Semester Study Abroad program in the fall of your second year. Is that right?

Eri: That's right. Actually, that's one of the biggest reasons I chose to study at this department. Could you tell me some of the things that you think are important when I try to improve my English skills?

Professor: Well, I can make some suggestions but, before I answer your question, why don't you tell me your ideas first?

Eri: Umm, I think grammar is important. Also, you need to have enough vocabulary.

Professor: Is that all?

Eri: Well, good pronunciation is important too, I think.

Professor: It sounds like you're thinking about only the language knowledge side of learning English.

Eri: It does? Uh, what do you mean? Are you saying I'm missing something more important?

Professor: Well, I think you're missing something that's as important as the things you just mentioned. Let me tell you a technique that will be useful when you try to communicate with other people in English.

Eri: If it helps with communication, it sounds very interesting. Please tell me.

Professor: All right. First of all, you don't have to be talkative when speaking in English, but you must try to give as much information as you can to the person you're speaking to.

Eri: How much? Can you be a little bit more specific?

Professor: Well, I usually tell my students that they should try to provide five times more information as they normally do when speaking Japanese.

Eri: Five times more? Well, I still don't quite get it.

Professor: OK. Let me give you an example. When someone asks you "What movies have you seen lately?" do you answer only by saying "Ghost in the Shell"? This is what I call a 'one-question, one-answer' exchange. Try to avoid this because it forces the other person to ask more questions to keep the conversation going. Also, this type of answering is what young children often do.

Eri: Well, I think I know what you mean. It sounds very childish if a college student answers that way.

Professor: Now that you understand what I was hinting at, how would you answer the same question?

Eri: OK. This is interesting. Umm, I saw a movie called Ghost in the Shell about a month ago. Since I'm a big fan of Scarlett Johansson, I was really looking forward to watching it. The movie was as good as I had expected. If you haven't seen it yet, I really recommend it. I'm sure you'll love it.

Professor: It sounds like you've got it. Great! That's not *talkative* but *informative* and that's how a good conversation goes between adults.

Chapter 2

English Communication (2)

Professor Saiki and Eri are still talking about useful techniques for communicating in English.

Professor: OK Eri, let me give you another interesting tip that is useful when communicating in English.

Eri: Yes, please do.

Professor: Do you know that Japanese people use two types of "Yes" in their conversation?

Eri: Two types of "Yes"? What do you mean?

Professor: Well, try to remember a recent phone conversation you had with one of your friends.

Eri: Yes, I was talking with another member of the Drama Circle just before I came to your office.

Professor: Can you remember how often you said "Yes" to show your friend that you were listening to them?

Eri: How often? I'm not sure, but quite a lot. It seems a natural way to talk.

Professor: I know. Actually, I do that too, when I talk with Japanese people. As you say, it's a natural conversation technique. I call this an 'attentive yes'. It shows we are listening, or paying attention. There is also the 'affirmative yes'. That shows you agree with the other person. "Yes, I think so too." The attentive yes only shows that you're listening. It doesn't necessarily mean that you agree with the other person.

Eri: I see what you mean. Does English also use two types of yes?

Professor: That's a very good question. As far as I understand, English speakers do not use the attentive yes when listening to others. As children, they learn to be more talkative, more active in conversation. On the other hand, Japanese children are taught to listen to others attentively rather than to talk a lot in conversation. So, Japanese use the attentive yes to encourage other people to keep speaking, but when English speakers say "yes", it is always only to show agreement.

Eri: That sounds very interesting.

Professor: So, there are two important points that will be very useful when you communicate with people in English. First, if you do not agree with what other people say, do not use the attentive yes. It could confuse them. Try to say "yes" only when you agree.

Eri: That's easier said than done. I'm used to using the attentive yes without thinking. It will be very difficult to stop.

Professor: Yes. It is difficult, I know, but I'm sure you can, if you concentrate. Oh, I have to go to a meeting in ten minutes, but very quickly, let me tell you the other important point. Don't be surprised or confused if English speakers do not use the attentive yes in conversation. My experiences tell me that they often listen to you very carefully but without saying anything. They show their attentiveness, not by saying "yes", but mainly by using facial expressions and body language.

This is their way of showing their attentiveness. I know it's difficult, but you can do it. Well, I hope these points will be useful as you practice to improve your English communication skills.

Eri: Yes, they are very interesting and helpful. Thank you very much for your time and expertise.

Professor: My great pleasure Eri.

Chapter 3

Studying Abroad

Eri goes to Professor Saiki's office to ask him about studying abroad.

Eri: Professor Saiki, I'm thinking of studying abroad while I'm a university student. In the future, I'd like to get a job that uses English. I know that you studied abroad when you were at university. Could you tell me about your experiences?

Professor: All right. When I was a student, I had the opportunity to study at a university in the U.S. as an exchange student. I stayed there for two years. It was a long time ago, but I still have many good memories of it.

Eri: For two years? Wow, you stayed in the U.S. for a long time. Did you have a good time?

Professor: I had good times and bad times.

Eri: Oh, you had bad times, too? What kind of problems did you have?

Professor: When I went to the U.S., the exchange rate between the American dollar and Japanese yen was very different. The yen was not as strong as it is now, so I didn't have enough money. I always thought about how to save money.

Eri: I see. I've heard that the American and Japanese governments agreed to set the exchange rate at 360 yen for one American dollar, to help the Japanese economy recover from destruction caused by the war. I know it was bad timing and not easy to study abroad at that time. Was there anything else?

Professor: Well that was the case before I went to America. At that time I was quite young, so when I got ill I felt very homesick. It was one of the hardest things I ever experienced. I wanted to go home to meet my family and friends in Japan. This often happens when someone studies abroad. Also, I missed Japanese food very much.

Eri: It sounds like you don't want me to study abroad, right?

Professor: No, no, please don't get me wrong. If you really want to study English and if you have the time and money, you should go to an English-speaking country to improve your English and to make your ambition a reality.

Eri: Thank you for your encouragement. I don't have enough money now, but I'm trying to save by doing part-time jobs. If I can study abroad, which country do you recommend?

Professor: Well, I recommend the U.S. because I know how exciting the life there is through my own experiences, but it's just my personal opinion. However, I'd like you to think about other countries too. Do you know other English-speaking countries?

Eri: The U.K., Canada, Australia. Do you have any other countries in mind?

Professor: Ireland and New Zealand. Also, in Southeast Asia there are Singapore, Malaysia and the Philippines. The Philippines is becoming a popular destination to study English.

Eri: The Philippines? Do they speak English? I think their native language is Tagalog.

Professor: Well, they have two official languages. One is Filipino, which is based on Tagalog. The other is English. More than 95 percent of the population can speak English in the Philippines.

Eri: Wow! How can I choose a country from among so many choices?

Professor: Well, you should take various points into consideration, for example cost, safety and cultural attractions.

Eri: I see. Could you tell me more?

Professor: Well, generally speaking, the U.K. and the U.S. are popular countries but expensive to live in. Canada and Australia are also popular and they are a little cheaper. The Philippines is much cheaper and closer to Japan than other countries, but all of these countries have both cities and nature.

Eri: Thank you for your time. Let me think about the advantages and disadvantages of each country carefully.

Professor: That's good! I hope that you'll take interest in non-English-speaking countries, too.

Chapter 4

The Necessity of English

Eri is asking Professor Saiki about why the English language is so important.

Eri: Professor Saiki, many people say that English is necessary for the global society. Why is it so important?

Professor: That's a good question. Let's think about it. Do you know how many people and countries there are in the world?

Eri: The world population is about 7 billion and there are about 200 countries. Is that right?

Professor: That's correct. The world population has been increasing and is now about 7.4 billion. Japan recognizes 196 independent countries, though the United Nations has 193 official member nations. So your answers were close. Well done! How many languages are there in the world?

Eri: I have no idea about that. Is it about 200 or more?

Professor: Actually, many more than you think. Some linguists, experts of languages, say that it's about 3,000. Other people think that it's about 6,000 to 7,000. Can you believe those numbers?

Eri: That's unbelievable! That can't be right! The number of languages is very much higher than the number of countries. Japan has only one language:

Japanese. Does the number of languages include dialects?

Professor: Good point! Actually, it's difficult to distinguish a language from a dialect. That's why we can't agree on the number of languages.

Eri: Ah, I see. Now I understand why the number of languages is much more than the number of countries.

Professor: Good. Do you know which language has the largest number of native speakers?

Eri: Oh I know that! It's Chinese!

Professor: Yes, it's Mandarin Chinese. So which language has the *second* largest number of native speakers?

Eri: English!

Professor: Perhaps. It may be English, Spanish or Hindi. It depends on the data you use. You can probably imagine how difficult it is to check the exact number of native speakers for those languages. So which is the most widely spoken language worldwide?

Eri: English?

Professor: That's right! It's spoken not only by native speakers but also by non-native speakers. There are about 4 hundred million native speakers of English. Then there are about 1.4 billion people who speak English as a second language or learn English as a foreign language worldwide. In total, it's approximately 1.8 billion people.

Eri: Wow! That's about a quarter of the world's population.

Professor: That's right! So if you can use English, you could communicate with 25% of the world's population.

Eri: Now I understand why people say English is so important. I also hear that English is the most used language on the Internet.

Professor: Yes, it is! Interestingly, Japanese is also often used on the web because a lot of Japanese can access the Internet. However, while Japanese is an official language only in Japan, about 60 countries have English as an official language. Again, if you can use English, you can communicate with so many people in the future.

Eri: Thank you for explaining that so clearly. I've learned enough to understand how important English is.

Professor: English is important, yes, but I'd like you to know another important thing about languages: If any one language becomes too dominant for international communication, it can create problems. I'm sorry, but I don't have enough time to explain now. Maybe next time?

Chapter 5

The Dominance of English

Professor Saiki and Eri are talking about the problem of the dominance of English as a language for international communication.

Eri: I've been concerned about something since we talked the other day.

Professor: What's the problem? Are you having trouble with a relationship, your studies or something else?

Eri: I'm worried that many Japanese people are still not so good at English. In Japan, we spend a lot of money every year on English education, but Japanese people don't seem to improve their English. Japan is becoming a popular tourist destination these days, maybe because of the upcoming Olympics. The number of foreigners coming to Japan has increased recently. We should be able to speak English, to show our hospitality to them. What do you think about that?

Professor: I'm surprised that you're so worried about this. I'm glad that you have a wide perspective as a university student, but I have to disagree with you. Actually, this is what I wanted to explain when we talked last time, but I didn't have enough time. Do you remember we discussed the importance of English the other day?

Eri: Yes, of course. I learned a lot. Thank you for explaining it so clearly.

Professor: You're welcome. Now I have enough time, let's think about why Japanese have to speak English to foreigners who visit Japan. They are not all

English-speaking people. Why don't you try to speak Japanese to them first?

Eri: Well, I don't think foreign people can speak Japanese, so I think it is kind of us to speak English to them. It's an international language. To explain about Japan to foreigners, we should try hard to learn English. Then we can communicate well with visitors to Japan.

Professor: I understand your point of view. You are studying English hard, so you should be able to communicate well using English. I think that's great!

Eri: So what's the problem?

Professor: What worries me is that some Japanese feel bad when they can't communicate clearly in English in Japan. Don't you think that's weird? We live in Japan, and our official language is Japanese. I think it's natural for foreign visitors to try to speak Japanese when they come here.

Eri: Well, let me think. I don't think it's strange because foreign people can't speak Japanese easily. For smooth communication we should take one step closer to them by speaking English. Japanese is a difficult language to learn, isn't it?

Professor: I don't think that's necessarily true. In my opinion, Japanese is as difficult, or as easy, as English. Japanese seems very difficult, especially to Westerners, maybe because it has three types of letters: *hiragana*, *katakana* and *kanji*. The writing system gives foreigners the impression that Japanese is difficult.

Eri: So you're saying that reading and writing Japanese is difficult, but that listening and speaking are not so difficult?

Professor: That's right. If foreign visitors try to learn conversational Japanese, they will probably see that it's not so difficult.

Eri: I see. That sounds persuasive.

Professor: Also, I'd like foreign people to learn our culture. I believe that learning a host country's language helps you to learn about its people and culture.

Eri: "When in Rome, do as the Romans do." Is that what you mean?

Professor: Exactly! When I go to foreign countries, I try to communicate in their language. Also, I often try their local foods and customs.

Eri: I understand what you're saying, but if you don't communicate well with foreign people, you can't help speaking English, right?

Professor: I have to agree, but I want those who study English to know one important thing. That's the problem with the dominance of English.

Eri: What do you mean by "the dominance of English"?

Professor: In international communication today, English is the most widely used language, as we discussed the other day. The global spread of English gives it the dominant status. I'm worried that the dominance of English causes serious problems. Linguists point out that the dominance of English causes linguistic and communicative inequality. One of the problems they highlight is that people who can speak English well discriminate against people who can't. This is one of the points that I'm worried about.

Eri: That sure sounds like a problem.

Professor: I hope that you'll respect all cultures and languages equally. Also, I don't want Japanese people to feel sorry or anxious that they can't speak English well in our own country.

Eri: I'm slowly starting to understand. So, I don't have to study English hard?

Professor: I didn't say that. People who need English for their future should study English seriously. I know that in the future, you want to get a job that uses English, so you have to study English as much as you can.

Eri: Oh, you're very strict.

Chapter 6

Culture and Civilization (1)

Eri goes to Professor Saiki's office to talk with him during his office hour.

Professor: Oh, hi Eri. How are you today?

Eri: Um, very well thank you. I hope I'm not interrupting you.

Professor: No, not at all. It's my office hour now. Come in and make yourself comfortable.

Eri: Thank you. I appreciate the way you make students feel welcome and relaxed.

Professor: Oh, thanks for the compliment. Well now, how can I help you?

Eri: Um, it's difficult for me to understand what 'culture' means. I couldn't understand your explanation in the previous class. At the end of the lesson you said that "judo is no longer part of traditional Japanese culture." I'm confused!

Professor: Well, I didn't say that exactly, though I said something very similar. I said "judo is no longer *just* part of traditional Japanese culture." I meant that judo is now part of a larger world heritage. I wanted to give a more detailed explanation, but I ran out of time at the end of the class, so I planned to explain it more in the next lesson.

Eri: Yes, you said so at the end of the class, but I can't go to the next lesson because I'll be attending a Buddhist memorial service for my grandfather. So, I'm

17

here to ask if you can explain it to me now.

Professor: Sure! I'd love to. OK, first of all, let's agree that judo is, and will always be, part of traditional Japanese culture. Right?

Eri: I certainly hope so because I'm a judo black belt.

Professor: Oh, are you? That's fantastic! You should tell me more about it some other time. Anyway, to better understand what 'culture' means, we should understand what 'civilization' means. Remember I said that judo is now part of a larger world heritage? That's another way of saying that judo is an example of civilization.

Eri: Hmmm. When I hear the word civilization, I think of Egypt, Mesopotamia and Greece, but you're not talking about those ancient civilizations. Am I right?

Professor: Exactly! My idea of civilization is different. Let me give you some other examples. Cars, the number zero and the moist hand towels Japanese call *oshibori* are all part of our civilization.

Eri: *Oshibori?* What does *oshibori* have to do with civilization?

Professor: Well, the service of giving *oshibori* to passengers on airplanes was started by Japan Airlines in 1954. Did you know that? This service is now provided by most of the world's airlines. Can you tell me one thing that is common to cars, the number zero and *oshibori*?

Eri: Well, let me see. From what you just said about *oshibori*, something they all have in common is that they are used everywhere.

Professor: That's right. They were invented in one country, then spread around the world and are now used in many countries. The extent that something is shared between countries is called the 'penetration rate'. It decides where an item is on the Culture-Civilization Scale.

Eri: The higher an item's penetration rate, the more widely it is shared between countries, so the more it is part of civilization. Am I right?

Professor: That's correct. As for the number zero, one book says that it was first discovered in India in the 7th century. It really changed mathematics. Now, every child over five years old understands the number zero if they have learned simple mathematics at school.

Eri: I think the number zero is a good example of civilization. Also, cars with gasoline-powered engines were invented in Germany at the end of the 19th century and the car has been used, changed and improved in many countries since then.

Professor: That's good! You seem to understand what I'm trying to say.

Eri: Yes, I think so. One other thing that all three things have in common is that they are all convenient. That's why people everywhere use them.

Chapter 7

Culture and Civilization (2)

Professor Saiki and Eri are still discussing culture and civilization in his office during office hour.

Professor: There is another important criterion for thinking about civilization. Have you heard of 'intercultural refraction'?

Eri: No. What does it mean?

Professor: Well, first understand that cultural items usually stay inside their cultural boundary and within the group that made them. So, what happens when an item from one culture is transplanted into another culture?

Eri: Well, you used the word 'refraction'. In physics, that means the change in a wave's direction. So, I think 'intercultural refraction' means that a cultural item is changed when it is transplanted into another culture.

Professor: Very good. You're smart.

Eri: Thank you. It was a lucky guess.

Professor: The smaller an item's intercultural refraction level, the *less* it changes across cultural boundaries so the more it is an item of *civilization*. The higher an item's refraction level, the *more* it changes across cultural boundaries, so the more it is an item of *culture*. The number zero is a good example. Wherever it is used, the number zero is always the same. It doesn't change. So, it has a refraction level of 0. It's a good example of civilization.

Eri: If you give me an example of an item that changes, perhaps I can understand cultural items.

Professor: All right. How about judo? It experienced at least two major changes to become accepted worldwide. At the Sydney Olympics in 2000, the blue *judogi* was used for the first time.

Eri: Yes. My mother told me that was the year I started practicing judo with my father. I was a cute, little, one-year old girl.

Professor: Is that right? I suppose you didn't wear a *judogi* at that time, huh?

Eri: No. I only wore a diaper when I practiced. I've always loved wearing the white *judogi* because white represents purity of the mind. I never wanted to wear the blue one.

Professor: Many Japanese judo practitioners at that time opposed the introduction of the blue *judogi* because they thought replacing pure white with impure blue was offensive.

Eri: I think I know how they felt. A color's meaning can change from one culture to another. Each cultural group should be allowed to preserve its traditional culture of color.

Professor: I understand and agree with you. So, why did the International Judo Federation introduce the mandatory blue *judogi*?

Eri: I'm not sure.

Professor: Because it helps the judges, referees, and spectators to distinguish one competitor from the other, so it's easier to judge and referee the match, and more exciting and fun for the spectators.

Eri: I see. So, Japan's cultural preference for white was overruled for practical reasons, so that judo succeeded in becoming an international sport?

Professor: Precisely! Another change in judo was the use of weight divisions. It was introduced at the Tokyo Olympics in 1964. You practice judo Eri. Can you tell me one of judo's central ideas in relation to weight divisions?

Eri: Um, you mean *ju yoku go o seisu*? Gentleness controls hardness.

Professor: Yes. Exactly! If you fight directly against a more powerful person, you will lose, but if you adjust and evade their attack, they will lose balance. Then you can defeat them.

Eri: Yes. It's the image of a small person throwing a big person.

Professor: This image of *ju yoku go o seisu* is easier to see in the open-weight class. The idea is that weight divisions make judo fairer, but it has also reduced the importance of *ju yoku go o seisu*. This is another change necessary for judo to become accepted in other countries where the idea of fair play is very important. This is why wrestling and boxing, which come from Western countries, also use weight divisions. So, a cultural item often has to change to become widely accepted by the international community, to become an example of civilization.

Eri: Ah, now I understand intercultural refraction. Thank you.

Chapter 8

The Importance of Presentation Skills

Eri is talking to Professor Saiki. She is nervous about giving a presentation

Eri: In some of my classes I have to give a presentation. I haven't given many before, so I'm really nervous, especially immediately before the start. I'm also afraid of embarrassing myself during a presentation. What should I do?

Professor: I understand how you feel. I know it's difficult to speak in public, but you're a university student now. You can't avoid it. If I explain my experiences and give you some basic tips for English presentations, maybe you can relax a little.

Eri: Thank you very much! You are always kind to students.

Professor: Oh, thank you for the compliment. Well, my first experience of public speaking was during my university seminar class. Like you, I didn't want to speak in public. For my first academic presentation, I decided to do just *two* things: be *confident* and make *lots* of eye contact with the audience.

Eri: Just two things? Were they enough to give a good presentation?

Professor: Yes. It worked well. I got very positive comments from my peers and the audience. Also, this successful experience made me realize that confidence and the willingness to communicate are very important.

Eri: I see.

Professor: Also, remember that you need to change from a self-centered view to an audience-centered view. See things from the audience's perspective. Thinking like this, my fear of public speaking gradually became a willingness to communicate. Also, the purpose of a presentation is not only to give information to the audience, but also to help them to understand that information.

Eri: How?

Professor: Well, we often forget that an audience is a group of people. They don't just receive information like an iPhone voice recording app. They *think* about that information. So, it's important to explain your message clearly. It's the same when we're having a conversation.

Eri: So, how do we do that?

Professor: I'll tell you three techniques that I use. First, make the presentation *comprehensible*, so it is easy to understand. Next, use body language *naturally* to support your meaning. Finally, tell a story.

Eri: How do we make a presentation comprehensible?

Professor: Oh that's easy! Use simple language. Don't use difficult or technical words. Don't use long sentences or difficult grammar. Next, your presentation must have a message, but keep the message *simple*. Don't include too many ideas. Also, explain your main points clearly during the presentation. Well-designed slides can really help.

Eri: Thanks for explaining 'comprehensible'. I'm gradually starting to understand.

Professor: Good. The second technique is to communicate with the audience using *natural* body language. Body language helps to send our message, so use it effectively. Body language includes smiling, natural gestures, posture and eye contact. These all help the audience to understand your information and your message. They also show your confidence and willingness to communicate.

Eri: I understand. The third point was to tell a story. What do you mean?

Professor: Well, good presentations explain your message through a story. The story helps you to connect with your audience. They feel closer to you because the information is more personalized. Also, it's easier to understand the presentation because the information is clearly organized and understandable. Your message becomes more interesting and easier to remember. I noticed this technique when I watched other people's presentations. Giving a presentation by telling a story has become popular in recent years.

Eri: Hmm. I'll try those techniques. If I use them, I think I can give a good presentation. Thank you for explaining them so clearly. You must be good at giving presentations.

Chapter 9

Travel and Tourism

Eri is knocking on Professor Saiki's office door.

Eri: Hello? Professor Saiki? May I come in? I'd like to talk with you for a few minutes.

Professor: Sure, please come in. What's up?

Eri: We're going to have a long vacation soon. What do you think I should do during the vacation?

Professor: Yes, there *is* a long vacation coming soon. Of course, as a university student, you should continue to study hard, even during the vacation.

Eri: Oh, I see. Any other ideas?

Professor: As I always say, you should read as many books as possible when you're young. You can learn a lot of interesting new things and it refines your Japanese. What do you think about that idea?

Eri: I know you love to read. Nobody reads as many books as you, as far as I know, but I'd like you to give me other ideas for the long vacation.

Professor: Well, I really do like to read, it's true. Anyway, let me think of some other ideas. Let me see. I advise you to experience the things you cannot do in your daily life. Have you heard the phrase "Experience is the best teacher"?

Eri: No. What does it mean?

Professor: Well, for example doing a part-time job, participating in volunteer activities or going to a driving school. I think there are many advantages to these experiences. Above all, I recommend you travel while you're young.

Eri: Now you're talking! I'm really interested in traveling. What should I keep in mind when planning a trip?

Professor: Are you thinking of a domestic or overseas trip?

Eri: It depends on the cost. I don't have much money, but I'd like to go overseas if it isn't too expensive.

Professor: Well, domestic travel isn't always cheaper than going abroad. Travelling in Japan can often be very expensive. Overseas travel sometimes costs less, depending on the destination. Anyway, let's begin with domestic travel. We have a lot of wonderful sightseeing spots in Japan. What are you interested in? Shopping? Hot springs? Amusement parks? Cultural attractions? Nature? Or something else?

Eri: I can't choose just one thing. Travel includes various activities. I wonder why traveling is so appealing?

Professor: Travel for pleasure is generally thought of as tourism. In tourism, you can see new sights, meet new people and try local cuisine. You can experience different cultures. I think that's why travel appeals to many people.

Eri: Hmm, I see. Why does traveling make me feel happy and refreshed?

Professor: Well, as you know, you grow physically as you get older. Your mind develops and expands through various experiences. Travel helps you to experience new and extraordinary things. So you could say "Travel expands your horizons" or "Travel broadens your mind". I think traveling makes you happy because you realize that you are broadening your mind. You can feel that you are growing mentally by experiencing new things.

Eri: I understand. Is it the same when I travel abroad?

Professor: Oh yes! Actually, traveling abroad helps you to experience new and extraordinary things much more easily because other cultures often do things differently. You speak good English Eri. You can communicate in English wherever you go in the world. As you know, English is the most widely used international language for traveling abroad. However, please also respect the local people, cultures and languages. If possible, try to communicate in the native language spoken wherever you go.

Eri: I understand. I promise I will.

Professor: Very good. Please enjoy your long vacation! Oh, just one more thing. Please remember that safety always comes first wherever you travel.

Chapter 10

Art Appreciation

Professor Saiki is talking with Eri in his office about how to appreciate art.

Professor: Now you are a university student Eri, you should have an interest in art to become an educated person.

Eri: I'm afraid I don't know much about art. I don't know how to appreciate it.

Professor: You shouldn't think of art as something difficult. It's not special at all. It is all around us, every day.

Eri: Really? What do you mean? For example?

Professor: Well, in general, fine art means things like paintings, sculptures, china and so on.

Eri: Did you say China? Why is China included in art?

Professor: OK. Let me explain what 'china' means. China is not about the country China, but about earthenware like plates, cups, vases, etc. It is called china because it was first made in China. For your information, lacquer ware is called 'japan' because it is thought to have come first from Japan.

Eri: You know a lot about this kind of thing, but I still think art is hard to understand.

Professor: Thanks for the compliment. It is said that "Age and experience teach wisdom". So, when you get older, you will become wiser, but of course you need to keep learning. Anyway, I know how you feel about art appreciation. However, if you think of art more widely, it also includes things like movies, music, and cuisine.

Eri: Ahhh, now it sounds more interesting. I like movies, music and of course food!

Professor: Yes, now you seem more interested. Don't worry about how you appreciate art. Each person has their own likes and dislikes. You can develop your own sense of beauty and your own personal preferences. That's all you need.

Eri: Really? I have likes and dislikes. Is it OK to follow my own opinions?

Professor: Yes, of course. That's my point. For example, classical paintings are usually included in art, but some people like modern paintings more than classical paintings.

Eri: I remember hearing that somewhere. Anyway, I'm relieved to know that I can appreciate art in my own way.

Professor: Well, it is said that fine art is a pleasure for the eyes, music is a pleasure for the ears and food is a pleasure for the tongue. When you eat something delicious, you should be interested in which ingredients are used, who cooked it and how it is cooked. The same thing is true for paintings, sculptures and other kinds of art.

Eri: So, if I'm interested in something, I should try to know about it in more detail. Is that what you mean?

Professor: Exactly! As the saying goes, "Beauty is in the eye of the beholder". It's up to you to decide what is good and what is bad.

Eri: I understand.

Professor: Just one more thing. I advise you to experience various kinds of art and performances, so I think it's a good idea to visit museums and theaters when you have time.

Eri: I see. Now I think I understand how to appreciate art. I will start to take an interest in it.

Professor: You should. As they say, "Art is long, life is short".

Eri: Thank you for sharing your ideas with me.

Chapter 11

Religions

Professor Saiki is talking to Eri in his office about religions.

Professor: I have a question for you Eri. Have you thought about religions seriously?

Eri: No, I haven't. I've learned that religious belief is a sensitive topic and that asking about a person's religion is impolite because it's too personal and private.

Professor: You're right. I understand your sensitive attitude toward religions. However, you need to know about religions in order to understand the world well.

Eri: Thank you for your suggestion. What do I need to know?

Professor: First, you should learn about religions in Japan. Which do you think has the largest number of followers in this country?

Eri: I think it's Buddhism. It's widely accepted in Japan. Am I right?

Professor: Well, yes and no. According to surveys, around 35% of Japan's population is Buddhist, though Buddhism doesn't come from Japan. It was founded in India and introduced to Japan through China and Korea in the 6th century. Historically, we learned a lot from the continent, but I'd like you to remember our indigenous religion. What's that?

Eri: You mean Shinto? Does it have a large number of followers?

Professor: Well, that's a difficult question to answer. Most Japanese people pray to their ancestors and worship gods at Shinto shrines. However, that doesn't necessarily mean that they are followers of Shinto. People who participate in Shinto ceremonies or rituals can be thought of as practitioners of 'Folk Shinto'. However, some of them don't think they are religious. Shinto is polytheistic and doesn't have a specific founder or holy book. So, it may be accepted in a flexible way in Japan.

Eri: That may sound unique to foreign people. How about other religions, for example Christianity? Do we have a lot of Christians in Japan?

Professor: Not so many, perhaps about 2%. There are more Christians in Korea. Also, as an Asian country, the Philippines are unique because more than 90% of its population is thought to be Christian.

Eri: That sounds interesting. Talking about Asia, I'd like to know about religions popular in China. Is Buddhism popular there too?

Professor: As far as I know, Buddhism, Taoism, Christianity and Islam have a certain number of followers, but in fact Chinese folk-religions, non-practicing and atheism are the most common.

Eri: Is Confucianism still popular in China?

Professor: That's a good question. People sometimes discuss whether Confucianism is a religion or a philosophy. Confucianism, Taoism and Buddhism make up the 'Three teachings'. People believe that these philosophies have influenced Chinese culture very strongly.

Eri: Which religion has the largest number of followers?

Professor: No-one knows the exact numbers, but if we add the estimated number of followers that each religion announces, then the total number is much higher than the world population.

Eri: Why does that happen? Are they lying?

Professor: No, I don't think so. Probably, they want people to think that their religion is the best. Japanese shrines and temples do the same thing when they announce the number of visitors on New Year's Day. They tend to overestimate. Anyway, let's get back to the topic. The largest religious groups are Christianity, Islam, Hinduism and Buddhism. Each religious group can be divided into groups called 'sects' or 'schools'.

Eri: I see. It's interesting to learn about religions. I'm curious about religions that Japanese people don't know so well, such as Islam and Hinduism.

Professor: Good. That's the spirit! Just one more thing! Foreign people sometimes wonder why some Japanese celebrate their children's birth at a shrine, get married at a church and have funerals at a temple. Some Japanese may think of such special days as memorial events. We may take different religious rituals in a very flexible manner as our ancestors worshipped *Yaoyorozu no Kami* or 'a myriad of gods' flexibly.

Eri: That's certainly true. Thank you as always.

Chapter 12

On Cultural Relativism (1)

Eri is asking Professor Saiki about the meaning of 'cultural relativism'.

Eri: When I visited a Southeast Asian country last summer, I saw the local people were living on the bank of a river. I saw a girl washing her hair with soap, a woman washing rice and boys playing. They were all in the river at the same time doing their own thing. As you may know, the rivers in Southeast Asia are muddy and to me it didn't look clean. According to cultural relativism, I should understand, accept and maybe even respect their lifestyle without judging them by my own cultural standards. Is that right?

Professor: I hope this hasn't been worrying you for too long. Anyway, I think there are two solutions to this problem. One is to have a clear understanding of what culture is *not*. The other is to ignore cultural relativism completely. Which would you prefer?

Eri: I'm not sure.

Professor: Well, let's discuss the second solution later. Let me explain the first one now.

Eri: Yes, please. I wish I had asked you about this much earlier.

Professor: Do you think that the things you saw in Southeast Asia are part of their culture?

Eri: Yes. It seemed to be their culture or their way of life for generations. I never thought that it might not be part of their culture.

Professor: If you assume that their lifestyle comes from their culture, then by cultural relativism you should see it as undeniable and acceptable, even if it is not so admirable when judged by your own cultural standards. However, if the things they are doing seem *so* strange or uncomfortable to you that they become unacceptable, you will be unsure about it. You will ask "Is it OK or not OK?"

Eri: Yes. That's exactly what I've been thinking about. I can't say that they should keep their lifestyle as it is now only because it's their culture, particularly when it seems unhealthy or dangerous.

Professor: Here's the first solution to the problem: Do not think of that lifestyle as an example of culture. If that is no longer culture, then you don't have to accept it or respect it. You could refuse it.

Eri: But if that wasn't culture, what was it?

Professor: Well, I assume that they were using the river water for most of their daily activities, maybe except for drinking. If they had enough clean, easily accessible water, do you think they would still use the river? I don't think they would. So, why did they use the river water?

Eri: Because they have no choice. Poverty forces them to use whatever is available.

Professor: That's correct. We should never mix up culture with poverty. Those daily activities are not part of their culture if they are abandoned when other ways of doing something, for example getting clean water from a faucet, become available. This is something we talked about as an example of civilization before, remember?

Eri: Yes! I remember. Well, thanks to you, I feel much better now. I understand more clearly that what I saw was not an example of their culture but a way of life due to poverty.

Professor: However, can you think of any situation where we might have to consider that lifestyle as an example of culture?

Eri: What do you mean? We've just solved the problem, haven't we?

Professor: Well, there is one case where their daily activities in that river must be considered part of their culture. When they believe the river is a sacred or holy place where gods or Buddhist nature might live.

Eri: Oh, like the Ganges in India? I've heard that Indian people, particularly Hindus, believe the waters of the Ganges are both pure and purifying.

Professor: That's right. Similarly, if the Southeast Asians you saw believe that their river is sacred, then their behavior is cultural and should be considered respectable, if you agree with cultural relativism.

Eri: Yes. If it is related to their religion, I would feel less uncomfortable, but I would still worry about their health. Anyway, I'm feeling much better now. I really appreciate your time and expertise.

Professor: My great pleasure as always.

Chapter 13

On Cultural Relativism (2)

Eri is still talking with Professor Saiki about cultural relativism.

Professor: I said there are two solutions to your problem. The first was to think that the things you saw in Southeast Asia are *not* examples of culture, but the result of poverty. Let's talk about the second idea: completely ignoring cultural relativism.

Eri: Yes. It sounds very interesting, but I feel bad to completely ignore what has been taught at school for so long.

Professor: Well, maybe you think that you *must* follow cultural relativism, but don't worry. It is said that "Everything is relative, nothing is absolute". People may not always need to rely on cultural relativism when we have contact with different cultures. Actually, Japanese people are inherently relativistic in their character. It might be better if we didn't use cultural relativism.

Eri: Why?

Professor: Well, an important point in cultural relativism is that a person's beliefs, values, and customs should be understood based on their own cultural criteria, not by the standards of other cultures. We should tolerate diversity. This is very similar to the Japanese idea of *junin toiro*. This translates into English as 'So many men, so many minds'. We should value our own culture's ideas and use them, rather than relying on someone else's.

Eri: So when we have our own ideas, for example *junin toiro*, we wouldn't need to use Western ideas. That's very interesting. Are there other reasons why it might be unnecessary for Japanese people to use cultural relativism?

Professor: Another reason relates to patterns of communication generally used in Japan. It is often said that the main goal of social interactions in Japan is to achieve and maintain harmonious or conflict-free relations, even if only superficially. So, we usually try to agree with opponent's opinions or feelings, while not telling our own.

Eri: I see. I think that's true when we talk with people more senior in social status or age and even when we are with friends of the same age.

Professor: This communication pattern is called 'Comparative Assimilation'. It helps people with different ideas to coexist. For example, Japanese people often answer both yes and no to a question: Yes is their 'public face', while No is their 'true intention'. This is *tatemae* and *honne* that Japanese are famous for.

Eri: Now I understand why you think Japanese people have a relativistic character.

Professor: You do? Good. Can you explain?

Eri: I'll try. When you talked about people with different ideas coexisting, I thought of 'tolerance for diversity'. Then the two ideas overlapped.

Professor: Very good. Cultural relativism and Japanese people's comparative assimilation patterns of communication have the same purpose. They both help people with different ideas to coexist. The other communication pattern, which Japanese people *don't* like to use, is called 'Exclusive Assimilation'.

Eri: Exclusive, not comparative?

Professor: The exclusive assimilation communication pattern doesn't allow two different things to coexist. The answer to a question must be either yes or no. There is no middle. Greek logic calls this 'The Law of Excluded Middle'. Japanese like an ambiguous statement because it can be thoughtful of other people's feeling. However, people who come from cultures that use the exclusive assimilation pattern of communication avoid ambiguous statements. They are more open and direct. Most native English-speaking cultures generally use this pattern of communication.

Chapter 14

On Cultural Relativism (3)

The discussion on cultural relativism between Professor Saiki and Eri continues.

Eri: So native English-speaking cultures like to communicate directly using the exclusive pattern of communication! That's why our English teachers often tell us to explain our ideas directly when speaking or writing in English.

Professor: That's right! Next, let's think about 'ethnocentrism'. This means that people see their own culture, ethnicity or country as better than others. It can be a serious barrier to smooth intercultural communication. Mild ethnocentrism can give us pride in our own culture, but...

Eri: ...but if it is too much, the result can be racism. That's scary. Ethnocentrism is part of human nature, but I think it's stronger in some people than others and in some cultures than others.

Professor: I agree. I have an idea about the relationship between ethnocentrism and the exclusive pattern of communication.

Eri: You suggested before that they are structurally the same, like cultural relativism and comparative patterns of communication.

Professor: That's correct. As I suggested before, native English-speaking people usually use exclusive patterns of communication. Therefore, I think that they are to some extent ethnocentric in character and because of this they adopted cultural relativism to avoid possible negative behavior like racism.

Eri: So cultural relativism limits the negative impact of strong ethnocentrism, for example, in the US where racial discrimination is slowly reducing.

Professor: That's a good example. Do you think relativistic Japanese will get a similar result from accepting and using cultural relativism?

Eri: No, I don't think so. If Japanese people are already relativistic, it doesn't seem necessary.

Professor: I agree. This is excessive acceptance of relativism by Japanese. It reinforces their relativistic way of thinking to a socio-pathological level. This is unfortunate, particularly for young people.

Eri: Pathological level? That means sickness, doesn't it? Could you explain that more clearly?

Professor: Well, we have talked about the comparative pattern of communication that Japanese often use. This helps to avoid conflicting ideas or opinions with others by matching our ideas with theirs. Cultural relativism, which encourages people to understand and tolerate other cultures, is used as a convenient excuse by Japanese people to avoid exchanging opinions and exploring the differences between us.

Eri: I know what you mean. I often hear my friends say "I respect your opinions", but they seem to have different ideas.

Professor: Today, cultural relativism is often thought to be necessary in understanding different cultures. I think that Japanese society generally encourages this way of thinking without considering the possible negative consequences. This situation is at a pathological level because cultural relativism taught in schools does not develop students' critical-thinking skills, particularly about bad or evil things. We have our own device: *junin toiro*. This is good enough for Japanese people to become mildly tolerant of diversity.

Eri: Thank you for your time and expertise. I really enjoyed talking with you.

Professor: Before you go, there's one more thing. When I said "native English-speaking people", I meant mainly white Christians. The Political Correctness movement has become stronger since the 1990's. Perhaps cultural relativism was promoted to weaken the status of white Christians, to destroy their culture and traditions. If so, we should be very careful about the real purpose of cultural relativism in our society.

Supplementary Reading

A Sound Historical Perspective

In this is conversation, Professor Saiki and Eri are talking about historical perspectives.

Eri: I want to ask a very important question. In your welcome speech at the entrance ceremony in April, you said we should be proud Japanese before we think about being international citizens.

Professor: Yes, I remember.

Eri: I like Japan because it's my home country and I'm proud of many traditional and modern things in Japan, but I have negative feelings about Japan's war history. Japan invaded other Asian countries and our soldiers committed mass killings. Even if the descriptions are sometimes exaggerated, with this history, how can I be proud to be Japanese?

Professor: Well, thank you for asking about this and about having an accurate historical perspective of the Second World War in Asia about 70 years ago. First of all, you should know that there are at least three different historical perspectives on the war. One is often called '*jigyaku-shikan*' or the 'Self-Tormenting Historical View'. Basically, this view says that Japanese people should feel guilty and apologize for the bad things Japan did between 1931 and 1945. This is the view taught in Japan's elementary and junior high schools since the end of the war.

Eri: You mean this is my perspective of Japan's war history? Yes, I guess so. This is the only reasonable historical view to accept, isn't it? I remember my high school history teacher saying "Don't believe people who say that Japan liberated Asians from the control of Western countries like Britain and America".

Professor: How interesting! Actually, that's the second historical perspective, called '*shokuminchi-kaiho-shikan*' or the 'Colonial Liberation View'.

Eri: Wait a minute. My high school history teacher taught that people who support that view are lunatics.

Professor: Well, I don't think I'm a lunatic. Think about it! Many Asian countries, for example Burma, India and Indonesia, became independent after the war.

Eri: That sounds like Japan invaded those countries to help them become independent. Is that really true? I was told something completely different: That Japan only did evil things everywhere they went during the war.

Professor: Do you know that about 2,000 Japanese soldiers fought with Indonesians against Holland and Britain after the war?

Eri: I didn't know that. Why did they do that?

Professor: Before the war, Indonesia was a British and Dutch colony. After the war, Britain and Holland returned to Indonesia to take back control. Indonesians fought for their independence. Japanese soldiers who stayed in Indonesia after the war helped the Indonesians by training them. Of the 2,000, about half died.

Eri: What? Really? The history textbooks don't tell us about that. This makes me feel better about Japan's war history.

Professor: That's good. Another thing about Japan's invasion of Indonesia will make you feel even better. The main Indonesian army that fought for independence against Holland and Britain after the war was made up of the former members of PETA, a volunteer army consisting of local Indonesian youth. Japanese volunteers from the occupying Japanese army established and nurtured this military organization.

Eri: You mean the Japanese army in Indonesia trained the Indonesian army? That's surprising! If that's true, why didn't the Indonesians use that training to fight against the Japanese army in Indonesia?

Professor: That's a very good point. Some minor riots were reported toward the end of the occupation, but basically the relationship between the Japanese army and the Indonesian people was cooperative, not hostile. The Indonesians actively welcomed the Japanese soldiers when they arrived in Java after pushing out the Dutch army.

Eri: That' very interesting. I didn't know much about World War II in Asia.

Professor: There are many other historical facts that will surprise you. Eventually, you will understand that much of Japanese history from the self-tormenting perspective is not supported by strong arguments and facts. You're lucky to have a lot of time to research this. It's something you should do as a university student majoring in International Liberal Arts.

Eri: Yes. I really want to know about Japan, the world and what really happened in the war. I want to be proud of my Japanese heritage and become an international person. Why weren't we taught these different perspectives at school?

Professor: Well, as I said before, if this is widely known, the *jigyaku-shikan* or Self-Tormenting View of History won't be accepted. It's that simple. It might surprise you, but there are groups who don't want Japan to be a strong country. They wrote an inaccurate version of Japan's war history and want us to teach it in schools to minimize nationalistic pride. I believe that no country can be strong and stable if its people don't love and have pride in it.

Eri: Hmmm. Learning our country's history is a lot more serious and complicated than I thought. You said there are *three* historical perspectives. One is the self-tormenting view and another is the colonial liberation perspective. What is the third?

Professor: OK, the third historical perspective. First, I must say that I disagree with the first perspective. It is also called the '*Tokyo-saiban-shikan*' or 'Historical View based on the Tokyo War Crimes Trial'. The official name of this trial is the International Military Tribunal for the Far East. The trial took two and a half years, from May 1946 to November 1948. Do you know anything about this important trial? Did your high school history teacher talk about it?

Eri: I don't remember. I think I've heard of it but I don't know about it. Maybe I shouldn't say this, but I hated the history teacher's class because he often said bad things about Japan. So, I didn't listen well or participate actively in his class.

Professor: That's too bad, but it's not your fault. Basically, the Tokyo Trial View of History says that the tribunal's judgments were valid and legitimate. All the military incidents and fighting with Japan, from the Manchurian Incident in 1937 to the end of the war in 1945, were a conspiracy by the defendants to conquer the Asia-Pacific region and that everything Japan did before and during the war was evil.

Eri: That sounds familiar.

Professor: However, some people say that this military trial was a show trial from the beginning because it had many weak points. For example, the judges were chosen by the US and other victorious countries. So, the Tokyo Trial is often seen as one-sided. Also, the trail was not based on contemporary international law.

Therefore, we can challenge the trial's validity. So, we need to know much more about the Tokyo Trial to fully understand why the historical view does not show the real story of those years. Also, after the war, Japan was under US-led allied occupation for nearly seven years. There were foreign soldiers in Japan. I hope you will study about this time of Japan's history too.

Eri: I certainly will. That sounds interesting, too. Now, please tell me about the third perspective.

Professor: OK. The third historical perspective is the one usually called the '*Kominterun inbo-shikan*' or the 'Comintern Conspiracy View of History'.

Eri: Conspiracy? That doesn't sound right.

Professor: I know what you mean. 'Conspiracy' doesn't sound academic or believable, but it hints at something important. I'll tell you about that later.

Eri: Well, what does 'Comintern' mean? I haven't heard that before.

Professor: It's the abbreviation for Communist International. It was an organization started by Lenin in Moscow in 1919 to promote communism. It ended in 1943. Lenin, then later Stalin, promoted revolution in other countries.

Eri: Was the *Nihon Kyosanto* or The Japanese Communist Party part of the Comintern?

Professor: Yes. The Japanese Communist Party was established in 1922 as the Japanese Branch of the Comintern and was controlled by Moscow. Anyway, an important point is '*haisen-kakumei ron*' or the 'Theory of Revolution through Defeat'. The basic idea was to start a communist revolution in the chaos after the war.

Eri: I've never heard of that either. So, I have two questions. First, why weren't we taught about this at school? Second, do I need to know a lot about communism to understand this conspiracy theory?

Professor: To answer your first question, I will just repeat what I said before: that *jigyaku-shikan* or the Self-Tormenting View of History, isn't valid if you understand the Theory of Revolution through Defeat.

Eri: That again?

Professor: Please research about communism later, but now it is enough to know that it is a political system adapted by the Soviet Union, China, North Korea and some other countries. They usually use a one-party political system, so the Communist Party controls the country. The people don't have many basic human rights, for example free speech and free worship.

Eri: That sounds terrible. Who wants such an inhumane system?

Professor: Nobody. Anyway, what they say in the context of the Theory of Revolution through Defeat is that Stalin's Comintern tricked Japan into wars, first with China, then with the United States.

Eri: So, the wars between Japan and China, and between Japan and the U.S. were both planned by Stalin? Well, it's hard to believe! How did he do that?

Professor: Directly and indirectly, Stalin sent many spies into Japanese and U.S. governments. Fumimaro Konoe was Japan's Prime Minister until just before the war started. His advisers believed in communism, openly or secretly, Ozaki Hotsumi for example. He had three political goals. Firstly, he wanted to help China become a communist country. Second, he wanted to prepare Japan to become a communist country. Third, he wanted to stop Japan attacking the Soviet Union. He did this by persuading Japan's government to start a war with the U.S. With Konoe's help, Ozaki succeeded in his first and third goals.

Eri: I haven't heard of Mr. Ozaki before, but from what you say, he was a very important person in Japan's prewar history.

Professor: Yes, a very important person. Meanwhile, the same thing was happening in the U.S. Many of President Franklin D. Roosevelt's close advisers were communists, including his wife, Eleanor Roosevelt. They influenced Roosevelt's policies. Why do you think the U.S. went to war with Japan?

Eri: Because of the surprise attack by Japan on Pearl Harbor. I know that much.

Professor: OK. Good. So, we can talk about how that attack became possible. One of President Roosevelt's top advisers was a man called Harry Dexter White. He was a communist and a Soviet spy. He is known for helping to write a document called the Hull Proposal. He included demands that Japan's government couldn't accept, for example that Japan leave China. Because of this proposal, the peace talks between Japan and the U.S. failed.

Eri: So, Mr. White and the communists *wanted* the peace talks to fail? Am I right?

Professor: Exactly! A famous American political commentator called Patrick Buchanan wrote that "FDR needed to maneuver Japan into firing the first shot". FDR is a common abbreviation for Franklin Delano Roosevelt. He knew the Japanese navy was near Pearl Harbor because the U.S. understood the Japanese navy's coded messages, but he didn't tell the U.S. navy in Hawaii.

Eri: So, the attack was a surprise, but actually it was not a surprise to Roosevelt and his advisors.

Professor: That's correct. To summarize, the Comintern wanted to start a revolution in Japan, so spies in the Japanese and U.S. governments persuaded those countries to go to war. Please research for yourself what happened after Pearl Harbor.

Eri: This third perspective is very interesting.

Professor: Before we end this conversation, let me explain why this historical view includes the word "conspiracy". The communists chose this name to trick people. They wanted to make people think this perspective was not credible.

編著者
竹野 純一郎（たけの じゅんいちろう）

中国学園大学国際教養学部　准教授
昭和44年生まれ
平成4年から18年間、岡山県公立高等学校で英語科教諭として従事
平成22年、兵庫教育大学大学院連合学校教育学研究科（博士号）取得
平成22年、中国短期大学英語コミュニケーション学科講師
平成27年、中国学園大学国際教養学部准教授
専門：学校教育学（英語教育）
著書：「"Hello" from Okayama 岡山から"ハロー"」（共著、山陽新聞社）、「英語好きな子に育つたのしいお話365」（共著、誠文堂新光社）

著者
佐生 武彦（さいき たけひこ）

中国学園大学国際教養学部　学部長／教授
昭和33年生まれ
昭和62年、サンフランシスコ州立大学スピーチ・コミュニケーション学部（修士号）取得
平成02年、中国短期大学英語コミュニケーション学科講師
平成22年、同上　学科長／教授
平成27年、中国学園大学国際教養学部　学科長／教授
専門：異文化コミュニケーション論、英語演劇
著書：「日本のむかし話オリジナル英語シナリオ集」Vol.1（単著、ふくろう出版）、「こころと文化」（共著、晃洋書房）、「アメリカン・ポップカルチャー　60年代を彩る偉人たち（共著、大学教育出版）

[JCOPY] 〈㈳出版者著作権管理機構 委託出版物〉

本書の無断複写(電子化を含む)は著作権法上での例外を除き禁じられています。本書をコピーされる場合は、そのつど事前に㈳出版者著作権管理機構(電話 03-3513-6969、FAX 03-3513-6979、e-mail: info@jcopy.or.jp)の許諾を得てください。
また本書を代行業者等の第三者に依頼してスキャンやデジタル化することは、たとえ個人や家庭内での利用であっても著作権法上認められておりません。

大学生のための国際教養ハンドブック
A Handbook of International Understanding for University Students

2018年4月15日 初版発行

編著者 竹野純一郎
著 者 佐生武彦

発 行 ふくろう出版
〒700-0035 岡山市北区高柳西町1-23
友野印刷ビル
TEL：086-255-2181
FAX：086-255-6324
http://www.296.jp
e-mail：info@296.jp
振替 01310-8-95147

印刷・製本 友野印刷株式会社
ISBN978-4-86186-713-2 C3082
©Junichiro Takeno, Takehiko Saiki 2018
定価は表紙に表示してあります。乱丁・落丁はお取り替えいたします。